95-1106

J
793.8
Fri

Friedhoffer, Robert
More magic tricks, science
facts

MORE MAGIC TRICKS, SCIENCE FACTS

FRIEDHOFFER,
THE MADMAN OF MAGIC

more
magic tricks,
science facts

**ILLUSTRATED BY
RICHARD KAUFMAN**

**PHOTOGRAPHS BY
TIMOTHY WHITE**

FRANKLIN WATTS ◆ 1990
NEW YORK ◆ LONDON ◆ TORONTO ◆ SYDNEY

Photographs courtesy of the author.

Cataloging-in-Publication Data

Friedhoffer, Robert.
More magic tricks, science facts / Friedhoffer, the Madman of
Magic ; illustrated by Richard Kaufman : photographs by Timothy White.
p.   cm.
Includes bibliographical references and index.
Summary: Presents several magic tricks that demonstrate principles
of mathematics, biology, chemistry, and physics.
ISBN 0-531-10969-0
1. Science—Experiments—Juvenile literature.   2. Scientific
recreations—Juvenile literature.   [1. Scientific recreations.
2. Mathematical recreations.   3. Magic tricks.]   I. Kaufman,
Richard. ill.   II. White, Timothy, ill.   III. Title.
Q164.F69   1990
793.8—dc20   90-37424   CIP   AC

To Annette Choynacki, who is
helping me solve the mysteries of life

ACKNOWLEDGMENTS

Thanks to the following people
for their help and encouragement:

Nikki Rae Friedhoffer, David and Faith Pedowitz,
Art Kahn, Rafael Bogarin, Timothy White, Richard
Kaufman, Jeanne Vestal, Iris Rosoff, Steve Mark
and Suzanne Phillips, Tony Andruzzi, Tom
Ladshaw, John Racherbaumer, Lee Freed,
Dr. Helene Mayer, the Helfands: Lonnie and
Jackie, Jeff and Marcia, Scott, Bernice, and
Sidney, Michael Chaut, Bill Stankey, Dave's Army-
Navy store, Brian Werther, Joel, Diane, Amanda,
Candice, and Douglas Druckman.

CONTENTS

"Any sufficiently advanced technology
is indistinguishable from magic."

Arthur C. Clarke
The Lost Worlds of 2001

"The magic of the past is
the science of the future."

Bob Friedhoffer

MORE MAGIC TRICKS, SCIENCE FACTS

A NOTE TO PARENTS AND TEACHERS

This book attempts to help children become interested in the study of the sciences while teaching them rudimentary principles. It does this by stripping away some of the mysteries associated with science and technology.

Scientific and mathematical principles presented as magic or puzzles have an allure that appeals to many children, even those with marginal scientific interests. This book was written to show children that science and math can be fun and exciting, as well as useful. It will:

- make the pursuit of science a game that children will want to play
- be a useful tool to children, allowing them to learn to express themselves in public through the performance of magic tricks
- help them to develop a knowledge of the psychology of working with people
- by the very nature of the performance, help them to learn to think on their feet

PREFACE

When my editor called to tell me that there was interest in a sequel to *Magic Tricks, Science Facts,* I was as happy as a kid in a toy store with a $2,000 gift certificate. I was being asked to continue a most enjoyable project, the combined study of science and magic.

Science had become a regular pastime with me. Wherever I turned, I kept on seeing articles on science and technology. A motorcycle magazine had an article on the physics of motorcycling. It discussed not only how the motorcycle went, but ways to make it go safer and faster. Newspapers and magazines had articles on the environment. They often described why the ecosystem should be maintained and improved. One magazine had an article on different adhesives and how they worked. I found this useful in assembling new magic tricks.

Not only did I find these articles interesting, I found them easier to understand with my ever-increasing knowledge of science.

I hope that your study of magic and science does not end with the reading of this book. Learning secrets of any sort is fun. I do hope that you enjoy the ones that you're about to read.

Bob Friedhoffer, aka
The Madman of Magic

INTRODUCTION

The performance of magic works because of "secrets." Magic is traditionally shrouded in mystery. If there were no secrets, magic would consist of *someone* standing on stage doing a bunch of "dumb things" that everyone knows. There would be no mysteries.

Keeping the secrets of magic to yourself is important if you wish to fool your audience. If the spectators are kept in the dark, they'll be impressed. If you tell them the secrets behind the tricks, *you* will be that someone standing on stage doing a bunch of "dumb things."

◆ ◆ ◆

This book was written as a *magic book*. Please help keep the secrets.

Before you perform any magic tricks successfully, you have to make a few decisions. You have to decide:

- ◆ that you want to do the trick

- that you're willing to spend some time learning the trick
- that you're ready to practice the trick until you can perform it well

Practicing the trick is the hardest part, but it is also the most rewarding. Diligent practice will allow you to fool your audience and keep you from worrying, "What do I do next?" while performing the trick.

◆ ◆ ◆

"As soon as the technical side of the trick is mastered, the student must turn to the dramatic, which is the most important as far as the effect is concerned." H. J. Burlingame, 1897

◆ ◆ ◆

To perform any of the tricks in this book, you should know if the trick you're about to do is based on science or math. If it's based on science, you must know which area of science—physics, chemistry, or physiology.

You must also consider the venue, or the area or place, where the performance is to take place. It can be either on stage or close to the spectators.

The tricks in this book are divided into four groups: physics, math, chemistry, and physiology. Each trick is broken into sections that give information on the effect produced by the trick, the props used, and the routine and method of performing the trick. There is also a follow-up note that further explains the science behind the magic.

These sections are described below.

EFFECT

When we watch a movie or TV show, we get so involved with the action that we forget that we are watching actors. We forget that we are just watching a story. For a while we actually believe that what's happening is real. That's what should happen to your audience, whether it's one person or fifty, when you perform a trick.

The effect is not what actually happens. It's what the audience *thinks* happens.

ROUTINE

This is the plot of the trick. When performing, you must tell some sort of story, even if it's done silently through pantomime. If the story is interesting, the audience will pay attention and enjoy your performance.

Most of the tricks in this book include a routine. This makes the mastering of the trick easier for you. A few of the tricks are given without involved routines. They are included so that you can develop a routine of your own.

PROPS

These are the items that you need for the performance. You must prepare the props, learn where they go in your performing area, and get used to handling them in a natural manner. If you don't prepare your props, the trick won't work properly.

Always handle your props with care. If they break, you won't be able to use them again.

Be careful when handling any chemicals. All of the chemicals recommended in this book can be handled safely, but must be treated with respect. Some of them can be dangerous if used in an improper or sloppy way.

METHOD

This is a combination of *effect, routine,* and *props.* When these are put together following the instructions in *method,* you end up with a magical performance.

NOTE

This section gives you a greater understanding of why or how the trick works. Included are some of the "real secrets" of science magic.

physics

A great trick with a borrowed cane

WEIRD
HANGING CANE

EFFECT

A walking stick or cane is placed next to your palm
and hangs there in a seemingly impossible way.

ROUTINE

Explained in *method.*

PROPS

A varnished wooden cane with a curved handle

METHOD

Borrow a cane or supply your own. One borrowed
from someone in the audience makes the trick seem
more impossible.

Hold your left hand as straight as possible with
your fingers pointing upward, the palm facing your
audience. With your right hand, hold the cane hor-

izontally, or parallel to the floor. Find the balance point, or center of gravity, between the handle and tip of the cane and place that point on the fatty portion of your left palm where the thumb attaches to the hand.

The cane will rotate a bit until the handle is angled somewhat behind your hand. When that happens, remove your right hand. The cane will remain suspended, hanging from your left palm.

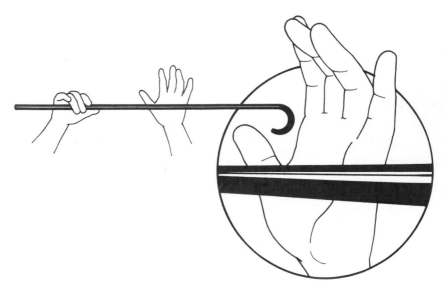

**Place the balance point on the fatty
portion of your palm**

After some practice, you will become so good at this that no one will notice that you're looking for the balance point. See the accompanying photo to clear up any doubts.

If your palm is barely moist or damp, it will be easier to perform this trick.

NOTE

The cane is actually balanced on a small ridge of flesh at the base of the thumb, but from the front it looks as though your hand is perfectly flat. There are two other reasons why this effect works:

1. Friction between your hand and the cane prevents the cane from sliding off. If the cane is varnished wood, you will find the trick easier to perform than if it were aluminum. The varnish will actually increase the friction between your hand and the cane.

2. The center of gravity of the cane is not where you might suppose. The bent handle, or crook, places the center of gravity at a position closer to the end than the center, depending upon the size of the bend.

Nate Leipzig, a well-known magician at the turn of the century, fooled everyone with this simple-to-perform suspension.

SOUND MASTER

EFFECT

You control sound in a strange manner.

ROUTINE

While sitting at a table, demonstrate how a tuning fork works.

Tap a tuning fork, causing it to vibrate. Let your audience hear the sound being generated. Tell them, "I've found a way to control the sound. I can project it anywhere I want. I have become *the sound master.*"

Cup your hand under the tuning fork's vibrating tines. Say, "I'm going to catch, focus, and project the sound waves." "Toss" the sound into a water glass on the table. Your friends will hear the sound coming from the glass. For variety, toss the sound into almost anything: a coffee cup, a flower vase, even a cereal bowl.

**Subtly touch the tuning fork
to the tabletop**

PROPS

a tuning fork
a water glass, coffee cup, etc.
a hard-topped wooden table, no tablecloth

METHOD

Examine the illustration to see how to hold the tuning fork with your right hand.

Proper grip of tuning fork

As you strike the tuning fork, make a grabbing motion at it with your left hand, as described in *routine*. Be careful not to touch the vibrating fork. If you do, the trick won't work because the tuning fork will stop vibrating.

When you tell the audience to look at the glass, move your cupped left hand toward the glass, then open it, letting the sound "spill out." At least, that's what you tell the audience. The secret behind the trick is that your right hand, still holding the tuning fork, has been resting on the table, the handle of the fork about ½ inch (1.28 cm) above the table-top.

As you open your left hand, touch the handle of the tuning fork to the tabletop. Be subtle about it.

The vibrations travel through the surface of the table and the sound appears to come from the glass. In fact, the sound is coming from the entire table-top, but since you directed the audience's attention to the glass, that's where it seems to come from.

NOTE

Notice how the sound of the tuning fork is louder when you touch the table with the handle of the fork. The tabletop becomes a soundboard and in-tensifies the sound. Soundboards are used in in-struments such as acoustic guitars, violins, and pi-anos.

INVISIBLE MOUSE

EFFECT

An invisible mouse performs at your command.

ROUTINE

"I've invented a method for making animals invisible. I started off small with an amoeba (a one-celled animal so small you need a microscope to see it). Then I went to something a little larger like an ant, and finally I succeeded in making larger animals invisible. I once made an elephant invisible, and the only way that I could find him was by the peanuts on his breath. Today I'm going to show you, in a manner of speaking, one of my best results with invisibility. It's a mouse."

At this point, gently display a stoppered opaque bottle and say, "Here it is, an invisible mouse."

Place the bottle on a table, remove the stopper, and talk gently to the mouse, just as you would to a real pet mouse. Next, take out a short length

The invisible mouse holds on for dear life

of clothesline and insert it into the mouth of the bottle. Speaking to the mouse, say, "Just grab the rope with your teeth and hold on."

Holding the rope in place, turn the bottle upside down. Then let go of the rope. Surprisingly, the rope remains suspended within the bottle.

Tell the mouse, "Good boy. Now, just hold it a little tighter."

Regripping the rope, turn the bottle right side up. Then let go of the bottle. The bottle remains suspended on the rope.

"Let go of it," you say to the mouse. Pull the rope from the mouth of the bottle, gently pour the mouse out onto the table, being careful that he doesn't run away. Hand the rope and bottle to your audience. Unless they're in on the secret, they will be unsuccessful in duplicating this trick.

PROPS

a small ketchup or soda bottle—either painted or totally covered with masking tape

a cork stopper large enough to close the mouth of the bottle

a piece of clothesline 12 inches (30.77 cm) long

a marble-sized Superball small enough to fit in the bottle

METHOD

The ball is in the bottle from the beginning. You won't lose it, because the stopper will keep it from coming out.

After you place the rope in the mouth of the bottle, hold on to the rope as you turn the bottle upside down.

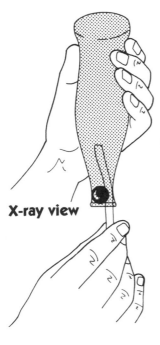

Wedging the ball between bottle and rope

X-ray view

The ball will fall somewhere between the inside of the bottle's neck and the rope. At this point, slowly pull on the rope, wedging the ball tightly between the rope and the neck of the bottle.

If you let go of the rope now, it will stay suspended from the bottle's mouth.

Next, turn the bottle right side up while holding onto the rope, and release the bottle. The wedged ball will hold the bottle securely against the rope.

To end the trick, push the rope in just a bit. This will allow the ball to fall to the bottom of the jar.

Hand the rope to your audience, and pick up the bottle by the neck, turning it upside down as you hand it out to your audience. The ball will fall into your waiting fingers, which close around it, hiding it from the eyes of the audience. When practicing this trick, do it over a bed or other soft surface, just in case the ball is the wrong size and does not hold the rope and bottle securely.

NOTE

This is a demonstration of friction. Friction is the resistance that arises from two surfaces in contact with each other. It is the force that an automobile's brakes use to stop a car.

HINDU
RICE TRICK

EFFECT

A jar full of rice clings mysteriously to an unpre-pared knife.

ROUTINE

As an introduction to the next effect, say the follow-ing:

"In India many years ago, Hindu fakirs (magi-cians) would do magic in the streets of Calcutta, performing amazing feats. One of the most famous tricks was done with a plain brass bowl and a quantity of rice. I don't have a brass bowl, so today I will use this glass jar.

"The fakir would let the audience examine the brass bowl and then fill it with rice." Let the audi-ence examine the jar. "Now that you're satisfied with your inspection, I'll fill the jar with rice." Do so.

"The fakir would stab a knife into the rice a number of times, utter a mystical chant, and amaz-ingly, when the knife was lifted, the bowl full of rice

The Hindu rice trick works

clung to it, being lifted high in the air." Demonstrate this.

"He would lower the bowl, remove the knife, pour out the rice, and let the audience once more examine the bowl, along with the knife and rice. The audience would not be able to discover the secret."

PROPS

a clean glass jar with a mouth narrower than its sides—see photo
1 pound (.45 kg) of uncooked regular rice, not instant
a dull butter knife

METHOD

Just stab the knife into the jar a number of times, packing down the rice, as in the above story, and the trick works by itself: the knife will stick in the rice. To release the knife, place the jar on a table, hold the jar securely with one hand, and twist the knife, which will release it from its grip on the rice.

You must practice this to learn how much "stabbing" is necessary. Surprisingly, this trick works equally well using a chopstick instead of a knife.

NOTE

The stabbing action initially packs down the rice. When the knife is jabbed in the final time, the rice holds the blade securely. At this point, the forces of friction are stronger than the force of gravity. When the knife is twisted, the rice is loosened a bit, packed down less tightly. Then the force of friction is less than the force of gravity.

SELF-INFLATING
BALLOON NUMBER 1

For safety reasons, you will need the assistance of a science teacher for this trick.

EFFECT

Balloons inflate magically. (A similar effect is found in *Self-Inflating Balloon Number 2,* but is accomplished by a totally different method.)

ROUTINE

Holding up an uninflated balloon, say to your audience, "Do you know what this is?"

After they tell you what it is, say, "There are two ways to inflate this balloon. The first way is to blow it up using your breath. The second way is by magic! I'm going to show you how to blow it up by magic."

Take out a drinking straw and display it to the audience.

Put the straw in your mouth, aim it toward the balloon, and start to blow through it. In a few seconds, the balloon inflates on its own, just as you said it would.

PROPS

rubber balloons
a large cardboard box—18 inches by 18 inches (46 cm by 46 cm), seal all the corners and edges of the box with strong tape
liquid nitrogen—difficult to get without the help of a science teacher; **very dangerous if not used with care**
leather or wool gloves

METHOD

Blow up the balloons by mouth and individually tie the ends. Place the balloons in the cardboard box.

Carefully pour enough liquid nitrogen into the box to cover the balloons to a depth of four to six inches. (Because the box has been sealed with tape, the liquified gas won't escape.) The balloons will start to shrink and will appear to be uninflated.

Using gloves, reach into the box and take out a balloon. Do not leave your hand in the liquid nitrogen for more than a second or two. At room temperature, the balloons will inflate to their original size.

NOTE

This trick utilizes the fact that gases compress when the temperature is lowered. The liquid nitrogen, which is extremely cold, will cool the air in the balloons, causing them to shrink.

Gas molecules are constantly moving. Pressure is created because moving molecules have kinetic energy. When the molecules hit the sides of a container in which the gas is held, they push on it. Lowering the temperature takes away some of the kinetic energy. Then the gas presses with less force on the walls of the container, in this case, the balloon. This is what causes the balloons to shrink when the temperature is lowered by the liquid nitrogen. Conversely, raising the temperature increases the kinetic energy, making the air in the balloons expand.

BENDING NAIL

EFFECT

A nail is bent by magic.

ROUTINE

A tenpenny nail, easily found in a hardware store, is displayed to your audience. They may examine it to their hearts' content.

Taking it back for a moment, you then let them examine a glass of water.

After they're satisfied that it's an ordinary glass, you place the nail halfway into the water, holding it with the fingertips of your right hand. Let them look at the nail through the side of the glass. The nail will appear to be straight.

Slowly pass your hand over the glass while uttering a magical incantation like "abracadabra." In a moment, the audience will see that the nail is now bent. Take the nail out of the water and let the audience look at it. Someone can even take it home as a souvenir.

PROPS

a clear water glass, filled with water
an ordinary tenpenny nail (construction nail about
    4 or 5 inches long)
a tenpenny nail with a slight bend, about
    15° in the center. You can make it by
    putting the nail halfway in a vice and
    gently tapping the side of the nail with
    a hammer. You can tell the degree of
    the bend by using a protractor.

the bent nail

METHOD

Place both nails in the right-hand pocket of your
jacket or pants.

Take out the ordinary nail and let the audience
examine it. Take it back and place it in your pocket
casually, while you display the glass of water.

Say something like, "Where'd I put that nail?"

Look for it, and then reach into your pocket,
taking out the bent nail. Without a pause, place the
nail so that half of its length is in the water at a 45°
angle. Make sure that the bent portion is angled
down, toward the bottom of the glass.

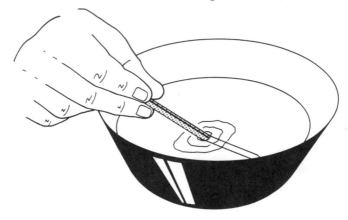

Refraction will make the nail appear to be straight if viewed from the side. Practice to learn the proper angle.

The fingers of your right hand slowly rotate the nail so the bend is now pointing at an upward angle. Let your audience view the nail for a moment, then pull it out of the water, and hand the bent nail over for examination.

NOTE

Refraction is the bending of light rays. When you place the bent nail in the water and hold it at the proper angle, refraction will make the nail look like it's straight. When you rotate the nail, refraction will make it look like it's bent at an angle greater than 15°.

Another example of refraction would be to hold an oar by its handle and place the other end into a pond or lake at a 45° angle, like you were rowing a boat. At the water line, the oar appears to be angled in an odd direction.

DISSOLVING
COIN

EFFECT

A coin vanishes in a glass of water.

ROUTINE

Say the following to your audience. Do the actions described here.

"Here's a coin, a handkerchief, and a glass of water. Examine them, so later on when I perform a miracle, you can't say that I've cheated.

"If I place the coin under the handkerchief, you know where it is, because you can see the outline of it under the cloth.

"If I place the handkerchief and coin over the glass of water, you can still see the outline of the coin under the cloth.

"I'll make it even easier for you. I'll let you hold the coin wrapped in the handkerchief. You know where the coin is, because not only do you see its outline, but you can also feel it."

The "coin" is under the handkerchief

"Now, drop the coin into the glass. I'll put the handkerchief over the glass, like so. Where is the coin now?"

The audience will answer, "In the glass."

Whip away the handkerchief, showing that the coin has vanished!

Hold up the glass for the audience to examine—it's empty except for the water.

To end the trick, slowly pour the water out of the glass and turn the glass upside down, proving that the coin has indeed vanished.

PROPS

a coin, either a half-dollar or a quarter

a glass disk, the same size as the coin. A replacement lens for a flashlight, available in a hardware store, is appropriate. Or ask a glazier or hardware store proprietor to cut a piece of glass for you

a glass filled with water; the inside bottom surface of the glass should be flat and the same diameter as the glass disk

a colored handkerchief that is not transparent; a bandanna is perfect

METHOD

Do the following before your audience arrives: Spread out the handkerchief on the table. Place the glass disc in the center of the handkerchief. Fold the handkerchief in half and leave it on the table.

Now you are ready to perform the trick.

Display the coin, then the glass.

While the audience is looking at the glass, reach into the fold of the handkerchief with both hands, your right hand holding the coin. Under cover of the cloth, place the coin into the palm of your left hand, covering it.

Pick up the handkerchief-covered glass disk by one edge with the fingers of your left hand.

Remove your right hand from the handkerchief. Grip the edges of the glass disk through the cloth with your right hand. (See photo.)

Take your left hand from under the handkerchief, concealing the real coin in your loosely held fist. Let your left hand drop down to your side.

Drape the handkerchief over the glass, the glass disk directly over the mouth of the glass.

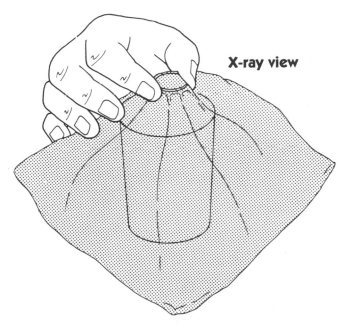

X-ray view

Have a spectator grip the edge of the glass disk through the handkerchief.

Have him drop the disk into the glass. He hears the coin drop into the glass.

Whip away the handkerchief. The coin appears to have vanished.

Slowly pour the water from the glass to prove that the coin has indeed vanished.

NOTE

The disk isn't seen on the bottom of the glass for a few reasons.

1. The disk is transparent, just like the glass.

2. The indexes of refraction of glass and water are closer than that of glass and air. That means it is harder to see glass underwater than in air.

3. When you pour the water from the glass, the disk should stay on the bottom. Surface tension of the water makes the disk adhere to the glass.

To prove that the index of refraction is similar for glass and water, put a glass plate inside a filled aquarium. The glass plate becomes practically invisible in water. One gag that you can do with this principle is to put a large circle of glass, about 6 inches (15 cm) in diameter, inside a 6-inch (15-cm) sewing hoop. Place the hoop with the glass insert in a filled fish tank, burying one edge of the hoop in the pebbles on the bottom of the tank.

Only the hoop will be visible in the water.

Offer a $10 reward to anyone who spots a fish swimming through the hoop.

People will look at it for a long time trying to win the reward, but your money is safe. The "invisible" glass prevents any fish from swimming through the hoop.

BLANK CARD PREDICTION

EFFECT

A prediction appears on a blank card.

ROUTINE

A blank plastic card is upright in the center of the cup. You bring out a plastic cup filled with water.

Ask the spectator to look at the card, while it's in the cup, and to say what she sees.

The response will be, "A blank card."

Now you say, "With the power of my mind, a word will appear on the card just seen to be blank. Not only will the word appear on the card, but I'll transmit that word to you telepathically."

The manner in which you say the next words is important.

"Concentrate!"

"Do you know the word that will appear on the card? Yes or no!"

If the presentation is practiced and perfected, the spectator will always say, "No!"

Remove the card from the cup. Printed on the face of the card is the word NO.

PROPS

an opaque plastic cup, found in many bath shops. The cup should have straight sides and measure about 3¾ inches (9.6 cm) high, with the mouth of the cup measuring about 2½ inches (6.4 cm) in diameter

a plastic card, constructed as follows: A plastic rectangle, cut so that it will stand upright within the cup, touching both sides and the bottom, and just as high as the top of the cup. Measure the inside of the cup and cut the rectangle accordingly.

a piece of mirrorlike contact paper

a piece of clear acetate about ⅟₆₄ inch to ⅟₃₂ inch, the same size as the plastic card

¼ inch Dennison brand sticky dots found in stationery stores

Glue the mirrored contact paper to the plastic rectangle and trim the excess.

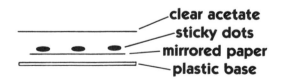

clear acetate
sticky dots
mirrored paper
plastic base

Spell out NO with the dots on the center of the contact paper, making sure that they adhere well.

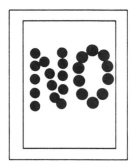

With a waterproof glue, attach the acetate to the mirrored contact paper. Just glue the edges. If the glue gets between the acetate and the contact paper, the trick won't work.

Waterproof the edges with a good waterproof sealer, hot melt glue, epoxy cement, etc. Make sure that it isn't too thick or the card won't fit into the cup.

When this is dry, place the card into the cup and fill the cup with water.

METHOD

The trick works by itself if you've constructed the card properly.

NOTE

When seen from the top edge, the word NO is invisible while the card is in the cup and underwater.

This happens because of refraction.

Refraction is the bending of light rays as they pass from one transparent medium to another. Different mediums have different indexes of refraction, or they each bend light at different angles.

There is a very small air space between the back of the acetate and the face of the mirrored contact paper. The acetate has a different index of refraction than the water and the air. These different indexes of refraction bend light rays. In the case of this trick, we experience what physicists call "total internal reflection." The light rays, coming from the dots underneath the acetate on the card, are bent and angled so as to be reflected back into the cup, and will not emerge from underneath the water. The underside of the water surface acts like a mirror.

Looking down into the cup, we actually see the reflection of the side of the cup instead of the face of the card.

The basic idea of this trick is from a European magician, Lubor Fiedler.

HEADLESS

EFFECT

A person's head disappears, then reappears.

ROUTINE

Say the following to your audience:

"Horror movies are fun, even though they're scary. I saw one not long ago where the bad guy was trying to transplant heads from one person to another. I don't know how they did it in the movie, but I've figured out how to do something like this on stage, using bloodless surgery.

"I need the assistance of a victim, er . . . that is, a volunteer from the audience."

Have the volunteer sit on a chair, facing the audience.

Tell the volunteer: "To protect the squeamish, I'm going to cover your head with a cardboard box."

Place a bottomless box on his head, so that it rests on his shoulders.

The head vanishes.
This wooden box is constructed using the
same 45° principle as described in the trick.

"We are going to do this magically, so we have no need for knives, scalpels, or saws. If you watch, you may actually see the head dematerialize."

Open the flaps in the front and back of the box.

"You will see that my helper's head has vanished."

Walk behind the volunteer. The audience can see you through the box.

Wave your hand behind the box. The audience can see your hand where the volunteer's head should be.

"I hope that I remember the proper way to bring the head back. I've been doing this trick for five years, and have had only one accident. That was last night!"

Close the flaps of the box, remove the box from your helper's head, and there he is, as good as new.

PROPS

corrugated cardboard (you can use cardboard boxes from supermarkets)
sturdy duct tape
2 sheets of Lucite® mirror, 14 inches by 17 inches each (36 cm by 44 cm)

Follow the directions below to construct the box (see illustrations).

Construct a bottomless rectangular box from the corrugated cardboard, about 15 inches by 15 inches by 30 inches (39 cm by 39 cm by 77 cm). Seal the edges with tape.

To give the box some strength, cut out a 15-inch-by-15-inch (38-cm-by-38-cm) piece of corrugated cardboard and attach it halfway in the box.

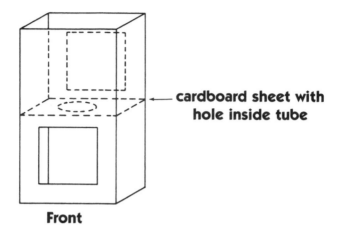

cardboard sheet with hole inside tube

Front

Before securing this partition, cut a hole about 7 inches (18 cm) in diameter in the center of it.

Now attach the partition.

Cut an opening in the upper, rear part of the box, about 10 inches by 13 inches (26 cm by 33 cm).

Cut an opening the same size in the lower part of the front of the box.

Cut two pieces of cardboard, 11 inches by 14 inches each (28 cm by 36 cm). Attach one piece of cardboard to the front of the box so that it covers the hole. Hinge it at the top so that it opens upward. Attach the other piece to the rear of the box so that it covers the rear hole. These flaps will act as doors to hide the mirrors in the box.

Place the sheets of Lucite mirror at 45° angles inside the box, one at the bottom, one at the top (see illustrations for placement). If the mirrors are placed properly, they will create the illusion that you are looking directly through the box. (Be careful not to dirty the mirrors, or the illusion will be ruined.)

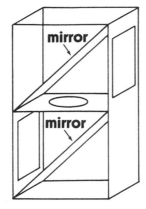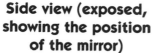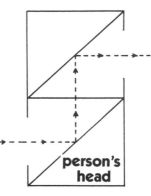

Side view (exposed, showing the position of the mirror)   **Side view (how the spectators' view bounces from mirror to mirror)**

It is not necessary to use a rehearsed helper as long as the person you select is a good sport and won't try to ruin the trick.

These measurements should work for most kids. If your assistant will be larger, just scale up the width and depth of the box. The mirrors must *always* be at 45°.

NOTE

This is a relatively new version of a very old trick.

You have created a periscope, much like that used on submarines or tanks. But, instead of prisms, as used in regular periscopes, you have used mirrors.

Light travels in a straight line. Therefore, the image from the back of the box hits the first mirror, which is at a 45° angle, and is reflected into the second mirror, which is at a reciprocal 45° angle.

The second mirror straightens out the path of light. It appears as though we are looking through the space where the assistant's head should be.

Normally, when we view an image in a mirror, we see a reversed image or mirror image.

As the image from behind the box is reflected into two mirrors, we get a true image.

math

VANISHING
LINE

EFFECT

A line vanishes from a sheet of paper.

ROUTINE

Draw ten parallel lines on a piece of paper. Cut the paper diagonally. Shift the paper slightly. One of the lines vanishes. Shifted back to its original position, the line reappears.

PROPS

a sheet of paper, 6 inches (15.38 cm) long by 4
    inches (10.26 cm) wide
a pencil
a ruler
scissors

METHOD

Draw ten parallel lines in the middle of the sheet of paper, ½ inch (1.28 cm) apart (see illustration). Each line should be about 3 inches (7.7 cm) long.

Cut the paper on the diagonal, corner to corner.

Align the two pieces of paper so that they are in their original, uncut position.

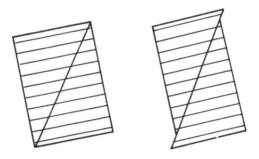

Have a spectator count the number of lines. There will be ten.

Slide the lower portion up and to the left, the width of one line, keeping the diagonal edge touching.

Have the spectator count the number of lines. He will now count eleven. Move the paper back to the original position and he will count ten.

NOTE

Martin Gardner, scientist, magician, and author, has called this line paradox the *Principle of Concealed Distribution*.

The line does not appear from nowhere. It is simply taken from other lines. You can prove this by first measuring the length of each line. They should all be 3 inches (7.7 cm) long.

When you cut the diagonal and slide the bottom sheet over, the lines should now be 3 inches long minus ⅑ of 3 inches, or 2.67 inches (6.85 cm) long.

THE TRICK THAT
FOOLED EINSTEIN

EFFECT

You make an accurate prediction.

ROUTINE

Take a deck of cards from your pocket and tell a friend that you're about to show her a trick that fooled Albert Einstein, the great scientist.

Ask her to shuffle the cards. Then have her take a few cards from the top of the deck.

Next, take a few cards from the top and place the rest of the deck aside.

Ask your friend to count the number of cards she's taken but to keep the number secret. She can do this by turning her back or by counting the cards underneath a table.

While she's counting, count the number of cards that you've taken, keeping the number to yourself.

When you're finished, say to her, "I have as many cards as you do, plus three more, and the balance that I'm left holding when added to yours will equal fifteen."

Ask her how many cards she has. Count out that number from the cards in your hand, plus three more.

Starting with the number your friend originally counted, count out the balance of the cards you hold. Amazingly, the total is fifteen.

Your prediction is accurate.

PROPS

a deck of cards

METHOD

To do this trick, you must first make sure that you take more cards than your friend. Try to make sure that you have at least six more cards than she does. You'll have to guess approximately how many she has.

Next, count the number of cards that are in your possession. When you know the number in your hand, subtract one, two, three, or four (it doesn't matter which) from the total, remembering this number and the remainder.

For example, if you've taken eighteen cards, subtract three, as in *Routine,* which will give you a remainder of fifteen (18 − 3 = 15). Remember the numbers 3 and 15.

The most important part of the trick is the wording of your prediction. The key to this trick is that all you're really doing is stating how many items you have in your hand, in a truthful but strange way. For example, consider this statement:

"I have as many cards as you do, plus three

more, and the balance that I'm left holding when added to yours will equal fifteen."

In this case, let's assume that your friend states that she has eleven cards. Count out eleven cards in your hand ("I have as many cards as you do"), then count out three more cards ("plus three more"): 11 + 3 = 14.

18 − 14 = 4. Balance left in your hand.

11 + 4 = 15. "And the balance that I have in my hand when added to yours will equal 15."

Once again, all you're doing is stating that you have a certain number of cards in your hand, but the way in which you say it makes it seem like a prediction.

This trick may be repeated.

Another example: Your friend takes twelve cards, you take twenty-two.

Now you can say, "I have as many cards as you do, plus four more, and the balance that I'm left holding when added to yours will equal eighteen," or "I have as many cards as you do, plus six more, and the balance that I'm left holding when added to yours will equal sixteen."

INSTANT ADDITION

EFFECT

Prove that you're a math whiz by instantly adding multi-digit numbers.

ROUTINE

Ask a helper from the audience to form four numbers of one to twelve digits each.

Challenge him to add these randomly selected numbers on a calculator. Before he has finished inputting the first multi-digit number, you will have mentally come up with the proper answer.

PROPS

a calculator or adding machine
twelve strips of cardboard printed with numbers (four to a slip), as follows:

STRIP NUMBER

1	2	3	4	5	6	7	8	9	10	11	12
7	3	9	5	4	7	2	7	5	8	5	2
6	9	7	9	5	6	7	2	7	6	4	9
3	4	8	6	3	8	4	8	9	7	2	5
5	6	2	4	9	5	9	9	6	4	9	7

METHOD

Ask your helper to take any number of cardboard strips and arrange them next to each other in any order. Then have him form four numbers of one to twelve digits each, using these strips. The numbers formed should run from left to right. For instance, taking strips 1, 2, 3, and 4 listed in the *Props* section, you can form two, four-digit numbers as follows:

1st example	2nd example
7,395	5,937
6,979	9,796
3,486	6,843
5,624	4,265

Give your helper the calculator and have him start to add up all of the numbers.

To come up with the correct answer, look at the third number from the top, then subtract 2 from the ones column and put a 2 in the column after the farthest digit to the left.

In the first example, this will give an answer of: 23,484.

The third number is 3,486; subtract 2 from the ones column. This will give you 3,484. Then put a

2 in the column to the left of the last digit on the left (the thousands column). This will give you 23,484.

The second example will give an answer of: 26,841.

The third number in the second example is 6,843. Subtract 2 from the ones column; this will give you 6,841. Then add a 2 to the left of the farthest digit on the left. This will give you the answer of 26,841.

NOTE

This routine, based on an idea by magician Theo Timmerman, is an example of a mathematical phenomenon known as matrix addition.

To impress and confuse your audience, tell them that there are over a million possible permutations (any one of the total changes in position possible in a group) and combinations (any combining of various parts of a group).

BOOK
PREDICTION

EFFECT

Predict a line from a book.

ROUTINE

Write down a prediction on a piece of paper, fold it in half, and place it on the table in full view of your audience.

Have an assistant from the audience perform some rather simple arithmetic, addition and subtraction, on a freely chosen three-digit number.

When she is finished, display the answer, which should be a four-digit number, to everyone in the audience.

The answer will be used to indicate a page number and a line number in a freely chosen book.

A free choice of either book

Bring attention to two books lying on the table and offer a choice of either one to your assistant.

When a book is chosen, have her open it up to the page arrived at by arithmetic, and count down to the line indicated. She should now read the line out loud to the rest of the audience.

Have your assistant pick up the prediction, open it, and read what is written. The audience will be totally amazed when the prediction is identical to the line just read from the book.

PROPS

two books
a piece of paper
a pencil

METHOD

The Prediction
Select a book that you would like to use for this trick—a book on ESP, a chemistry textbook, a novel, anything. Make sure that the book has at least 100 pages.

Turn to page 89 and count down to the tenth line on that page. Copy the first word or the entire line on the piece of paper. Fold the paper in half. This is your prediction.

The Math
Ask one person in the audience to make up a three-digit number—each digit being a different number (for example, 354). Let the person know that she can choose any combination of numbers.

Then ask her to reverse the order of the digits and subtract the smaller number from the larger (for example, 453 − 354 = 099). If the answer is two digits, include zero in the hundreds column.

Take that answer and reverse it (for example, 990).

Add the two numbers together (for example 099 + 990 = 1089).

If the directions are followed carefully, the answer will always be 1089.

The Book

Place the book from which you have made your prediction and another book on a table. The trick is to have your assistant select the book with the prediction, but make it appear as if the book were freely chosen.

You do this by saying to your assistant, "There are two books on the table. Push one of them toward me."

If the book she pushes is the one from which you've made your prediction, say, "That's fine. We'll use this one." Then pick it up and hand it to her.

If the book she pushes to you is the wrong one, say, "That's fine. I'll keep this one." Pick up the other book (the one with the prediction) and hand it to her.

This part of the trick is called "the magician's force" and is used by some of the finest performers in the world. If done smoothly, the audience won't realize that a free choice was not made.

At this point, bring the calculated number, 1089, to your assistant's attention once again. Explain how it represents the tenth line on page 89 of the "freely selected" book. Ask her to turn to page 89, read the tenth line, then read the "prediction."

If you practice the presentation of this trick, you will totally amaze your audience.

Be sure not to repeat this trick to the same group of people—someone might remember the number 1089.

NOTE

This trick proves that math has many strange quirks. This particular quirk was discovered by accident by a group of mathematicians while they were doing some calculations. Thanks to them, we can turn it into a terrific trick.

If you study math, you can find other equally interesting principles that you can turn into tricks.

CIRCUS
MULTI-PURPOSE BELTS

EFFECT

Paper belts torn in half react in strange ways.

ROUTINE

Say to your audience: "I'd like to give you some idea of what a circus sideshow barker would do to attract people to his show."

Pretend that you're a circus barker—be dramatic; ham it up. After all, you're putting on a show.

"Ladies and gentlemen, and children of all ages, step right up and I'll tell you all about the fabulous sideshow and its strange inhabitants."

Display three loops of paper, each about 2 feet (.61 m) in diameter.

"Each of these belts is the property of one of our fabulous attractions. Watch carefully.

"This first one belongs to our famous magician [name yourself], an ordinary person who likes to wear two belts at a time. If I cut the belt around the middle, we end up with two belts, each the same size.

"This next belt is for the Siamese twins, Yin and Yang. As I cut this belt in exactly the same manner as I did the first, you will notice that we end up with two belts forever entwined. A perfect piece of sartorial splendor for Yin and Yang.

"The third belt belongs to the biggest exhibit under the bigtop—the world's largest man, with an extra-large waist. You can see, of course, that this belt is of ordinary size until, using my magic powers, I cut the belt in the exact same method used the first two times. As you can see, the belt has now doubled in size.

"These, ladies and gentlemen, are only a small portion of the acts within our fine exhibit. Step right up and see them all."

PROPS

cellophane tape
scissors
3-inch-wide (7.7cm) paper. Adding machine paper
   works best. Or cut and paste newspaper to size.
   You'll need about 5 feet (1.52 m) of paper for
   each loop.

Using the paper, make three loops:

   ◆ a plain loop, the ends taped together

**Two
loops
separate**

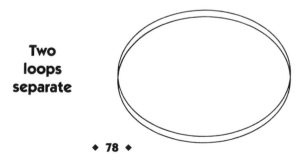

• a loop with a full twist, the ends taped together

**Two
intertwined
loops**

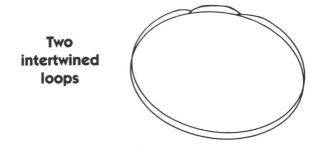

• a loop with half a twist, the ends taped together

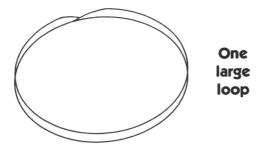

**One
large
loop**

METHOD

Cut each loop in half lengthwise. The tricks work
by themselves.

The plain loop, when cut, becomes two loops.

The loop with a full twist, when cut, becomes
two loops intertwined.

The loop with half a twist, when cut, becomes
a loop whose circumference is doubled.

EXPLANATION

These tricks are based on the principles of topology, a branch of mathematics that deals with sur-

faces. In topology, figures are changed into other forms by bending, stretching, and twisting.

By twisting a loop in this trick, you created a Möbius (mo-bee-us) strip, named for August Möbius, a nineteenth-century German mathematician. A Möbius strip is a one-sided surface.

This sounds strange, but it can be proven easily by taking a strip of paper with a half twist, its ends taped together to form a loop, and placing a pen point on the centerline, starting at the taped ends. Draw down the centerline, and you will find that when you again reach the taped section, the pen point is on the opposite side of where you started. Continue along, and you will find that when you reach the taped section the line once again connects to itself. You can learn more about Möbius strips and other oddities from books on topology.

chemistry

In the following section, many of the tricks involve chemicals that are dangerous to use, or can be dangerous if handled improperly. Use extreme caution when working with these chemicals. Do not get any of them in your eyes or mouth or on your clothing. Be sure that an adult assists you when you practice these particular tricks. *Caution* is the name of the game here.

SELF-INFLATING
BALLOON NUMBER 2

EFFECT

A balloon inflates magically.

ROUTINE

Holding up an uninflated balloon, say to your audience, "Do you know what this is?" After they tell you what it is, say, "There are two ways to inflate this balloon. The first way is to blow it up, using your breath. The second way is by magic! I'm going to show you how to blow it up by magic."

Take out a drinking straw and display it to the audience.

Put the straw in your mouth, aim it toward the balloon, and start to blow through it. In a few seconds, the balloon inflates on its own, just as you said it would.

PROPS

a large balloon, 10 inches to 12 inches (26 cm to
    31 cm) around
a drinking straw
a small test tube, filled with vinegar, lightly corked
½ teaspoon of baking soda

Prepare the balloon before your performance:
    Pour the baking soda into the balloon.
    Put the corked test tube in the valve of the bal-
loon, cork in.
    Tie the balloon closed.

METHOD

This trick is best done a little distance away from
your audience.
    Take out the prepared balloon and display it to
the audience.
    While handling the balloon, secretly dislodge
the cork from the test tube, allowing the vinegar to
mix with the baking soda. You need to practice this
action so that the audience will not notice the test
tube.

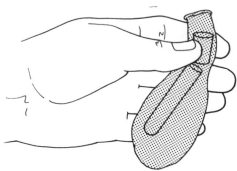

The cork is separated from the test tube

Blow through the straw. This is just some magical misdirection.

The balloon inflates automatically.

NOTE

The chemical reaction between the baking soda and the vinegar releases carbon dioxide (CO_2). The amount of carbon dioxide liberated from the reaction is enough to inflate the balloon.

This chemical reaction is used in an older type of fire extinguisher called a soda-acid extinguisher. You may have seen such a piece of apparatus in an old building. The soda and acid (probably hydrochloric) create a tremendous amount of carbon dioxide, which builds up and forces the water stored in the extinguisher out at a high pressure.

SCARY
THOUGHTS

EFFECT

Demonstrate how to get rid of scary thoughts and nightmares.

ROUTINE

Say the following to your audience: "I've invented a way to get rid of scary thoughts and nightmares. It sounds weird, but it works.

"First, you have to think the scary thoughts, even if you're afraid.

"Then make believe that you're catching them and throw them away.

"I'm able to catch my scary thoughts in a glass of water. Then I wash them down a sink. Once I do that, the thoughts never come back.

"I'll give you a demonstration right now."

Fill a drinking glass with water from a pitcher and set it on a table in front of your audience.

Stare at the glass, muttering, "Evil thoughts, begone." At the same time, make believe that you are picking those thoughts from your mind and tossing them into the water.

After you concentrate for thirty or forty seconds, the water turns inky, proving that your method really works.

PROPS

a 10-ounce (300 ml) drinking glass
a pitcher
the following solutions, mixed in separate glass
 containers:

Solution A
280 mg potassium bisulfate crystals
456 mg soluble starch
120 cc warm water
 Let cool. Pour into the pitcher.

Solution B
143 mg sodium sulfite anhydrous
182 mg potassium iodate (pure)
 60 cc warm water
 Let cool. Pour a small amount into the glass.

 These solutions work best if they are prepared within twenty-four hours of the performance.

Caution
Whenever you use chemicals, treat them with respect and be careful. Do not drink them or let anyone else drink them, get them in your eyes, or splash them on anyone.

METHOD

As you tell the story given in the *Routine* section, hold the glass at its bottom, so that solution B is hidden by your hand.

When the demonstration takes place, pour solution A into the glass, so that it mixes well with solution B.

Within thirty to forty seconds, the new solution will turn a dark, inky color.

Experiment with the amounts of solutions used to learn the exact timing of the reaction.

NOTE

This is an example of a chemical "clock reaction" and is based on a trick by magician Orville Meyer known as *"Think! Ink!"*

THE BONES OF
THE RUBBER CHICKEN

EFFECT

Chicken bones become so elastic that they can be tied into knots.

ROUTINE

Say the following to your audience:

"Lots of people have tried to be the life of the party by doing silly things—putting lampshades on their heads, doing lousy impressions, singing corny songs, doing magic tricks, even pulling out rubber chickens."

(For laughs, illustrate each "life of the party" stunt as it is stated, using props when appropriate.)

After you show the rubber chicken, ask the audience, "Do you know where rubber chickens come from? I'll show you. They come from real chickens that have been turned into rubber.

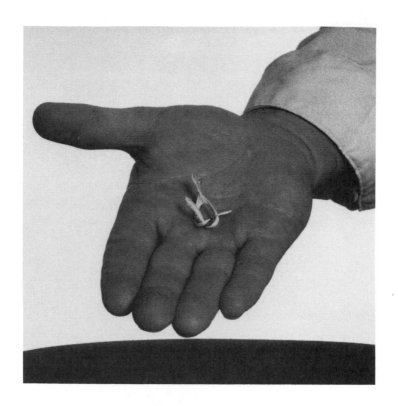

A rubber chicken bone tied in a knot

"I won't turn a whole chicken into rubber, but I'll do it to a chicken bone. Here's a wishbone from last night's dinner."

Place the bone under a handkerchief and say the magic words: "Worthless stone, whale blubber, chicken bone, turn to rubber."

Have a spectator remove the chicken bone from the handkerchief. He will find that the bone is now very elastic. He may even tie it into a knot without its breaking. This is proof that rubber chickens come from real ones.

PROPS

2 chicken wishbones, cleaned, equal in size
a handkerchief or bandanna
a jar of white vinegar

Prepare one of the wishbones by putting it in the jar of vinegar. Let it stand for twenty-four hours; then change the vinegar and let it stand for another twenty-four hours. At the end of that time, the chicken bone should be extremely flexible. If you like, you can tie it in a knot and let it dry. It will become hard and inflexible.

METHOD

While seated at a table, secretly put the "rubber chicken bone" in the middle of the handkerchief. Make sure that it's not noticed by the audience.

At the appropriate time in the routine, as outlined above, place the regular chicken bone under the handkerchief.

Under cover of the handkerchief, drop the regular bone into your lap.

Grasp the rubber bone through the handkerchief so that everyone can see it. The audience has no reason to suspect that a switch has been made.

Finish up the routine and let your audience see that the bone has become like rubber. Or you can let them examine the knotted bone.

NOTE

The vinegar reacts with the calcium in the chicken bone, changing the chemical structure and making the bone elastic.

physiology

TELLTALE
HAND

EFFECT

Read someone's thoughts.

ROUTINE

Tell a friend that you have been studying ESP (extrasensory perception) and that your psychic powers have started to develop.

Hand her two coins (for instance, a nickel and a penny), placing one in each hand.

Ask your friend to concentrate, thinking only of one coin. To help her concentrate, she must raise the hand with the thought-of coin to her forehead.

Before she raises her hand, turn your back so that you can't see her.

After a moment or two, ask your friend to hold both hands in front of her body, waist high.

When she has done this, turn around and gaze at her, apparently reading her mind. Then tell her which coin she was thinking about.

PROPS

2 coins of different values

METHOD

Place one coin into each of your helper's hands. Remember which coin is in which hand.

Tell your friend to keep her hands waist high until you turn around. When you turn, your friend should hold the hand with the selected coin to her forehead for fifteen seconds.

After she drops her hands to her waist, turn around and quickly glance at her hands. The hand that was held to her forehead will be paler than the other one.

All you have to do now is remember which coin was in that hand. Once you know the coin, hold your fingertips to your forehead, close your eyes, and pretend that you're truly reading her mind.

After a suitable pause, tell your friend which coin was on her mind.

NOTE

Gravity has pulled blood from the arm that was raised. To some small degree, the amount of blood under the surface of the skin determines the shade of color of your arm and hand. Since there would be less blood in the arm that was raised, that hand will appear paler than the other.

The complexion of the skin does play a part in the performance of this trick. The skin of a dark-complected person will not change color to the same degree as the skin of a light-complected person.

HEADQUARTER

EFFECT

Make a friend look silly.

ROUTINE

Say to your audience, "Would you like to see my headquarter?"

It's a strange audience that would deny themselves this thrill.

With great theatrical presence, take a quarter from your pocket and press it to your forehead.

When you remove your hand, the coin stays just where you placed it. At this point, tell your audience, "Time how long it takes for me to get it off."

Start to scrunch up and relax your forehead, keeping your hands cupped at your waist, so that when the coin falls off you can catch it.

Now ask one unsuspecting audience member if he would like to try it, and if he thinks he can do it faster than you.

When he says yes, take the coin and press it

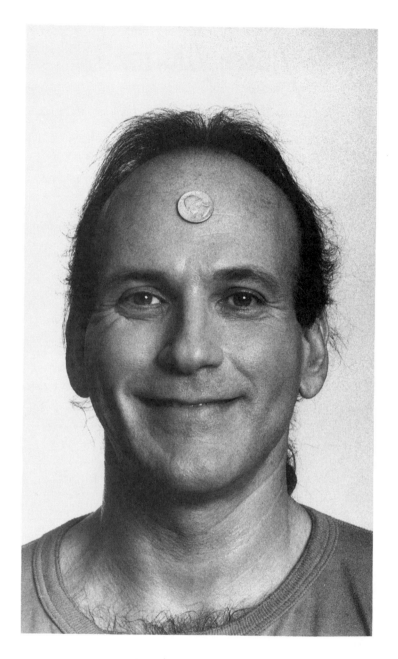

Friedhoffer's headquarter

on his forehead. After you press it to his skin, though, remove the coin without telling him. Take your hand away and nonchalantly put the coin in your pocket. Be sneaky.

"Now see how long it takes you to get the quarter off your forehead, without using your hands."

Your victim will make the wierdest faces for quite awhile before he reaches up to see why the coin doesn't fall. Until he does that, he won't know that the coin is gone.

This is a lot of fun to do with one person or with a group of people, as long as they don't tell the victim that the coin isn't there.

PROPS

a quarter
a small cup of water

METHOD

When you take the coin out of your pocket, place a drop of water on the side that you'll press to your forehead. The coin will adhere to your head because of surface tension and air pressure.

NOTE

This is an interesting demonstration of nerve receptor cells of the skin.

For some reason, these receptors are still activated for some time after the pressure is removed, and your victim doesn't realize that the coin isn't there.

These cells are called Meissner cells after the scientist who discovered them.

THOUGHT
TRANSFERENCE

EFFECT

Read someone's thoughts.

ROUTINE

Sitting around with a group of your friends, tell them that you can read minds. Offer to demonstrate your powers in the following manner.

Take out a dozen items—pennies, marbles, baseball cards, anything—from a small paper bag. Explain to your friends:

"I will leave the room in a moment, shutting the door behind me. All of you must decide on a number between one and twelve. To indelibly inscribe that thought in your minds, one of you will take that number of objects and place them inside the bag, folding the top over, so I can't see inside of it.

"Then place the other objects where I can't see them. You can put them in a pocket, in a drawer, or even sit on them.

"When you have completed this, tell me to come back into the room."

At this point, you leave. Your friends follow your instructions and you come back into the room.

Walk over to one person and ask her to concentrate on the number. Gently place your fingertips on the sides of her head, at her temples, as though you're going to read her mind.

In a moment, tell your friends how many items were selected.

PROPS

a dozen objects, as mentioned above
a small paper or cloth bag, large enough to hold
　　the items

METHOD

Sneaky folks that magicians are, for this trick you use a helper, commonly called a "confederate" (No! Not Robert E. Lee) or a "stooge" (No! Not Moe, Larry, or Curly). Be sure that no one finds out that you are using a stooge, or you'll look silly.

When you leave the room, your "helper" should be the one to remember the number of objects concealed in the bag.

When you come back into the room, go over to your helper, placing your fingertips on her temples. She should pretend to concentrate, clenching her teeth together. She should bite down the number of times to equal the number of items in the bag.

When she does that, you will feel a slight movement in her temples. Count how many times she bites down and you will have the proper number of items in the bag.

NOTE

This trick reflects the fact that many parts of the body are interrelated. Muscles, tendons, and ligaments from the jaw are connected to the rest of the head and neck.

Just remember that old song, ". . . the head-bone connected to the jawbone . . ."

CONCLUSION

Now you have a whole arsenal of magic tricks to fool your friends. These tricks may be performed one at a time or strung together to produce a complete magic show. Practice these tricks, and I'm sure that you'll fool everyone who sees them.

I hope that you've enjoyed reading this book and learning some of its secrets. In addition to learning about magic, I hope that you've also discovered that science can be interesting and fun.

SUPPLIERS

EMUND SCIENTIFIC CO.
101 E. Gloucester Pike
Barrington, NJ 08007-1380

Send for their free catalog.
It's filled with all sorts
of scientific apparatus.

FREY SCIENTIFIC
905 Hickory Lane
Mansfield, OH 44905

Ask your teacher to send for this
free science catalog. The request
must be on school stationery.

LOUIS TANNEN, INC.
6 West 32nd St.
New York, NY 10001-3808

Great magic store. Greatest magic
catalog. Catalog costs $8.50 plus
$2.50 postage. Mention you read
about them in Friedhoffer's book.

PAUL DIAMOND'S MAIL ORDER MAGIC
P.O. Box 11570
Fort Lauderdale, FL 33339

Good prices. Tell Paul that you
want his free price list. Mention
Friedhoffer.

ABRACADABRA MAGIC SHOP
Department C-448
P.O. Box 463
Scotch Plains, NJ 07076

$2.00 gets you a catalog and
a six-month subscription to
the monthly newsletter.

HANK LEE'S MAGIC FACTORY
125 Lincoln Street
Boston, MA 02205

Great magic store. Good catalog!
Inquire as to cost.
Mention Friedhoffer.

ABBOTT'S MAGIC CO.
Colon, MI 49040

Good catalog! Inquire as to cost.

ZANADU
772 Newark Avenue
Jersey City, NJ 07306

$1 for a great catalog.
Mention Friedhoffer.

FOR FURTHER READING

Gardner, Robert. *Science Experiments*. New York: Franklin Watts, 1988.

Goldwyn, Martin. *How a Fly Walks Upside Down*. New York: Citadel Press, 1979.

Macaulay, David. *The Way Things Work*. Boston: Houghton-Mifflin, 1988.

White, Laurence B., Jr., and Ray Broekel. *Optical Illusions*. New York: Franklin Watts, 1986.

INDEX

ABOUT
THE AUTHOR

Friedhoffer has studied magic for
many years, ultimately receiving a
"Doctor of Arcane Letters" degree
from Miskatonic University in
Arkham, Massachusetts. He performs
all over the United States at such
places as the White House, colleges
and universities, trade shows, nightclubs,
society functions, and television shows.
He lives in New York City.